The Runaway

A Parable: How God Feels About His Rebellious Children

Judith Vander Wege

Dedicated to Our Father God,
who loves his children even when they rebel.
*"I reared children and brought them up,
but they have rebelled against me, (Isaiah1:2)*

ISBN: 979-8-8693-0250-2
Company Name: Paper Wrights Printed in the United States of America,

Table of Contents

Chapter One
The Runaway

"I'm sorry, Mom. Please let me come back."

LuAnn sank into her chair as she recognized the voice. *How long had she waited for this phone call? yet dreaded it?*

"Where are you, Stephanie?" She stalled for time to think. How could she say 'no' to her daughter? Yet, it hadn't worked the last time, or the time before, or...

"I'm at the Post Office booth. I hitched a ride. Mom, I'm not on drugs anymore. I've been clean a whole two weeks. I promise it will go better this time."

LuAnn sighed. "You'd have to follow our house rules."

"Of course. I know that."

It seemed like deja vu. How many times had she heard this runaway promise to obey? The episodes of rebellion had begun at age thirteen: defiance, refusal to go with the family to church, sneaking out, smoking, and drinking.

Then at fifteen the disappearing acts began. LuAnn still had nightmares of calling the police to "please find my daughter!"

Two months before her eighteenth birthday, she'd called—like this time. LuAnn, over-joyed at her repentance, had said "Of course you can come back. We'll always love you no matter what you do." And she meant it. Life was beautiful—for a couple of weeks.

Then the symptoms of rebellion showed up again. When LuAnn reminded Stephanie of the house rule: "No pornography allowed in the house," Stephanie blew up.

"You're such a prude! How do you expect me to live in this jail? I'm not staying here."

She threw some things into a suitcase and stormed out of the house before LuAnn could think of what to do. Days later, she learned Stephanie had left with a boyfriend for places unknown.

LuAnn hadn't heard from her for three years since then. But a friend had heard gossip from a friend and felt compelled to share it with LuAnn. It was not a pretty picture.

****

*****

Think about this:

What does God say about rebellion?

____

"Even the animals—the donkey and the ox—know their owner and appreciate his care for them, but not my people—They have cut themselves off from my help" (Isaiah 1:3-4 LB). How did Stephanie cut herself off from her mother's help?

____

In Luke 15, Jesus tells of a Prodigal Son who asked his father for his inheritance, (in essence saying, "You're as good as dead to me, so give me what I have coming."

Then he "squandered his wealth in wild living." In his subsequent poverty, he decided to go back and ask his father to forgive him and hire him. Did that go well? What did his father do?

How do you think that father felt about his son's rebellion?

How is that story similar to Lu Ann's and Stephanie's?

How would you feel if your children left home, cut themselves off from your help, and refused to come back, not allowing you to help them out of the mess they had fallen into?

Let's look at Isaiah 1:2-3 again: *"Hear, O Heavens! Listen, O earth! For the Lord has spoken: I reared children and brought them up, but they have rebelled against me. The ox knows his master, the donkey his owner's manger, but Israel does not know, my people do not understand"* (Isaiah 1:2-3 NIV).

In Nehemiah 9:5b-16 the Levites lead the people in praising God. *"Blessed be your glorious name, and may it be exalted above all blessing and praise. You alone are the Lord. You made the heavens, the earth and all that is in them. You give life to everything and the multitudes of Heaven worship you,"* (Nehemiah 9:3-6 NIV).

Since God is the Lord and made the heavens and the earth and gave us all life, does he have a right to expect us to follow certain rules? Why or why not?

In Deuteronomy 4:1, God told the Israelites, *"Hear now, O Israel, the decrees and laws I am about to teach you. Follow them so that you may live and may go in and take possession of the land that the Lord your God is giving you."*

Lu Ann wished she could help Stephanie see that obedience is for our own good. But after the last rebellious episode, she had felt relieved she was gone. She's over 18, she thought. I guess it's okay for her to be on her own.

LuAnn kept praying, but went on with life. Now, she knew she had a decision to make. *Stephanie is 21, and wants to come back. What should I do Lord? Do I have to take her back?*

Would God take her back? Would you?

Prayer: "Dear LORD, forgive us for the times we have gone our own way, turning our backs on you, ignoring your rules, and refusing your love. Amen.

****

******

Chapter Two
Please, Believe My Love

"Come now, let us reason together," says the LORD. "Though your sins are like scarlet, they shall be as white as snow; though they are red as crimson, they shall be as wool. If you are willing and obedient, you shall eat the best from the land; but if you resist and rebel, you will be devoured by the sword." For the mouth of the LORD has spoken. (Isaiah 1:18-20 NIV).

Parable continues:

"Yes, I'll come get you." LuAnn picked up her car keys. *Will it go any better this time? Only God knows. I can only hope and pray. Please Lord, give me wisdom in dealing with her.*

The car's headlights picked up a bedraggled figure huddled beside the phone booth outside the empty Post Office. *How scraggly her hair looks...dirty, torn jeans. How can she be so dirty? and thin.*Stephanie stood up as LuAnn parked. "Stephanie, what happened?

"Nuthin,'" She mumbled.

LuAnn tried to hug her, but it was like hugging a board. She couldn't help but think, *"Robbed & plundered, trapped in holes..."* (Isaiah 42:22 RSV). After a warm bath and a meal, Stephanie seemed more relaxed, but sullen. She wouldn't say much to her mother about the past three years. LuAnn sensed it must be painful to think about it. "Why don't you go to bed," she said, gently. "We'll talk more in the morning."

Next morning, LuAnn tried friendly conversation, but Stephanie seemed unreachable, as if her real self were locked up in a secret place.

LuAnn sighed. *"Father, where's the little girl I used to read to and sing to, play with, laugh and talk with? What happened to her?*

In a gentle but firm tone, she reminded Stephanie of the house rules. "As long as you stay here, I expect you to do your share of the housework. No alcohol, drugs, pornography, or smoking is allowed in the house. No boyfriends in your bedroom. I'd also like to be kept informed of your whereabouts."

A flicker of resentment flashed in Stephanie's eyes; then she looked down and nodded.

Your eyes seem haunted. What are you afraid of, my daughter? Don't you know how much I love you? Why would I keep taking you back if I didn't love you? Believe it, please.

As the days went by, it gratified LuAnn to see Stephanie keep her room neat, help with meals, dishes, vacuuming and dusting. She saw no disobedience. Yet, she felt a barrier between them. It was as if her daughter were a robot, doing what she had to do, yet with no heart.

****

****

Dig Deeper:

How would you feel if your runaway came home without expressing repentance, seeming resentful under the surface although doing what you asked him or her to do?

____

Would you be at ease if you suspected she only pretended to agree with your values, and obeyed because of compulsion, not because she wanted to?

____

Isaiah 1:11-17 (Amplified OT) says that the Israelites were doing the things God had commanded them to do, yet God said: *"To what purpose is the multitude of your sacrifices to Me [unless they are the offering of the heart]? I have had enough of {them}."* Why didn't God appreciate their offerings?

____

What do the following scriptures say about obedience from the heart? *"These people come near to me with their mouth and honor me with their lips, but their hearts are far from me. Their worship of me is made up only of rules taught by men,"*(Isaiah 29:13 NIV).

____

What does this verse mean: "I desire mercy, not sacrifice, and acknowledgment of God rather than burnt offerings, (Hosea 6:6 NIV)?

____

What do you think God wants from you?

____

I believe God wants us to know him, to acknowledge his ownership and provision, to understand he loves us, and to trust him.

During the time when I was angry at God for not answering my prayers the way I thought he should, (see Rescued By God's Mercy), I thought I knew him. I still went to church, read the Bible and prayed.

However, if I really knew him, would I have thought he had abandoned me?

To know our Creator and Lord is to trust him so much that we are in harmony with him. It is to be totally yielded to his will, knowing that whatever he does is what is best for us.

To call Jesus Christ our "LORD" means to recognize his right to rule over us. He is our boss in the best sense, the one who has the right to tell us what to do. He earned this right first of all by creating us, secondly by providing for our rescue from sin's captivity by willingly dying on the cross to pay for our sins.

In our parable, did Stephanie trust her mom's love?

If she did, wouldn't she have talked with her about her problems?

Proverbs 23:26 says, *"My son, give me your heart and let your eyes keep to my ways,"* What does God want us to do?

"The sacrifices of God are a broken spirit; a broken and contrite heart, O God, you will not despise." (Psalm 51:17 NIV).

Joel 2:12-14 says: *"Even now,"* declares the Lord, *"return to me with all your heart, with fasting and weeping and mourning; "Rend your hearts and not your garments. Return to the Lord, your God, for he is gracious and compassionate, slow to anger, and abounding in love,"* What does Joel 2:12-14 say God is like?

____

____

Prayer: Thank you, Lord Jesus, for paying the price so we could be cleansed from sin. Help us learn to know you, to acknowledge your ownership and provision, to understand you love us. Teach us to trust you. Amen.

Chapter Three
Merciful Judgment

"If you have a willing attitude and obey, then you will again eat the good crops of the land. But if you refuse and rebel, you will be devoured..." (Isaiah 1:19-20 NET).

Parable Continues:

LuAnn's heart ached. She wanted a relationship with Stephanie, not simply duties done as if her daughter were her servant. She wanted her daughter to know the rules were made because of love for her. *There's even defiance in her compliance,* she thought.

Uneasiness grew in LuAnn as the days went by. One day while LuAnn prayed, the thought came to her that something was wrong in Stephanie's room. While Stephanie was in the shower, LuAnn followed her nose and found a half-filled ashtray and cigarettes in a dresser drawer.

She felt sick when she saw a pile of unacceptable magazines under the bed. Behind the stereo, a whiskey bottle. Almost as if an invisible hand led her, she opened the closet door and looked in a back corner. There she found a stash of drugs and needles.

With weak knees, LuAnn forced herself back up the stairs just before Stephanie came out of the shower. She collapsed into a chair and dropped her face into her hands. "Oh God," she prayed. "What should I do?"

About a half hour later, the door bell rang. LuAnn answered it, then squared her shoulders and proceeded down the steps to confront Stephanie, who sat on the floor painting her toenails. "Stephanie..."

LuAnn sat on the bed. "You haven't been following the house rules."

"Sure I have. I've done what you told me to," she said coldly, not meeting her eyes.

"No, you haven't." LuAnn told her what she'd found.

"You invaded my privacy! I can't believe you'd do that!"

Stephanie yelled. Her eyes blazed. She got up and slammed the fingernail-polish bottle down on the dresser.

With tears in her eyes, LuAnn said firmly, "You've broken the rules and have to suffer the consequences. I've called the police."

"Mom! How could you?" Stephanie grabbed her duffel bag and began to stuff things into it.

LuAnn motioned to the policeman who'd followed her down the stairs, and pointed to the closet. He examined the stash while Stephanie bolted for the door. Another policeman blocked her exit.

"You're under arrest for possession of illegal drugs young lady." He snapped handcuffs on her wrists.

"I hate you!" Stephanie yelled at her mother as the policemen took her away.

****

*****

"Come, let's talk this over! Says the Lord; no matter how deep the stain of your sins, I can take it out and make you clean as freshly

fallen snow. Even if you are stained as red as crimson, I can make you white as wool. If you will only let me help you, if you will only obey, then I will make you rich! But if you keep on turning your backs and refusing to listen to me, you will be killed by your enemies; I, the Lord, have spoken. (Isaiah 1:18-19 LB)

What were the consequences of Stephanie's disobedience?

____

Isaiah 1:18-20: In spite of all Israel's rebellion, was God willing to forgive?

____

Isaiah 1:25-26: What was God's purpose in judging Israel?

____

What is God's purpose in judging, or disciplining us?

____

God says, "I will thoroughly purge away your dross, and remove your impurities." (Isaiah 1:25 NIV).

____

Why did Israel need judging? (See Isaiah 2:6-8, 3:8-16, 5:4, 7-8, 11-13, 20, 24)

____

Do you see any similarities between Israel then and America today?

____

Do you know how precious you are to God? See Isaiah 43:4 and Lam.4:1.

____

Like Gold, you may have to go through many steps in order to become what your Creator meant you to be. Gold ore has to, first of all, be blasted out of a mountain, then crushed, ground, amalgamated, heated, soaked in cyanide, then melted so the dross can be removed. Then the gold is cast into bars, flattened, beaten, cut, and beaten again until light shines through. Then it is finally ready for lettering, gilding, and gold lace.

****

****

Parable Continues:

When LuAnn visited her daughter in the treatment center three weeks later, she marveled and rejoiced at the difference in Stephanie's appearance. Her clean and neatly combed hair hung over her shoulders. Her eyes, no longer furtive, looked searchingly into her mother's as if wondering if LuAnn would believe her, as if knowing she had no right to expect it.

"I'm sorry, Mom. Really sorry."

Deja Vu again. How long had LuAnn been waiting for this? She looked at the girl sitting on the bed facing her. Could she believe her this time? She wanted to, with all her heart. But it was hard.

Stephanie looked down at her hands, then up again at her mother. "But I'm not asking to come home this time. I just want you to forgive me for all the heartache I've caused you."

Stephanie cleared her throat, looking away with tears in her eyes.

"Honey, I love you..." LuAnn said, but stopped when Stephanie looked back and lifted her hand, looking her mother directly in the eyes.

"I'm asking if it's okay with you if I go to Teen Challenge. When Maria talked to me last week, I wanted what she had, joy and peace. She told me about Jesus, as if he is her best friend. And I guess he is, but so much more.... Anyway, when she prayed with me, it seemed like a prison door opened and I could walk out if I want.

"I do want to, Mom. I asked Jesus to forgive me. Now, I want to follow him. I know I have a problem with drugs and I want to get rid of it. Maria says Teen Challenge can help."

Overjoyed, LuAnn gave her permission. They discussed the details, then parted with the first genuine mutual hug LuAnn could remember for the past seven years

Prayer: Thank you, Lord Jesus, that you give hope to the hopeless and that you can change rebellious hearts. Forgive us when we don't obey you. Teach us to trust you more completely. Please convict us if we are rebelling without realizing it so we can confess to you and receive forgiveness. Amen.

Chapter Four
Teen Challenge

Teen Challenge, started by David Wilkerson in 1958, is known throughout the world for providing successful recovery programs. David, a country preacher in Pennsylvania, picked up a LIFE magazine one night and read a story about some boys in jail in New York City charged with murder. He burst into tears and felt burdened to go to New York City and help them.

He did go, ministered God's love to them and to many other gang members and, over a period of time, led many of them to Christ. Then he started Teen Challenge for the rescue and rehabilitation of addicts and alcoholics. You can read this story in The Cross and the Switchblade, Jove Books, New York, 1962.

Nicky Cruz was the head of the first gang he met, and he told his story of transformation in Run, Baby, Run published by Bridge-Logos.com. Later he became a well-known evangelist.

For information about teen challenge see tcusa@teenchallengeusa.com or call (417)862-6969.

Whether one is a rebellious teenager as in The Runaway, or an older person who loses the way and slips into a pit (as in Rescued by God's Mercy), God's mercy is still available.

As I wrote in my book, Rescued by God's Mercy, I felt overwhelmed by the mercy Isaiah spoke of, and became convinced God cares about us. He desires us to experience life abundantly. Even his judgment is merciful as it warns us to turn from our sin, thereby protecting us from what would destroy us. If we accept His mercy, he can work in our lives for good. Apparently, He considers us valuable enough to teach us to trust him.

Chapter Five
The Red Thread of Redemption

God presents his merciful way of Salvation in His Holy Scriptures, the Bible. His 'Red Thread of Redemption' reaches throughout the Bible to teach us the way and reveal God's heart. An excerpt from <u>Rescued by God's Mercy</u> follows, explaining The Red Thread of Redemption:

"Someone is coming!" This statement can bring joy and excitement, ---or fear.

Adam and Eve were afraid because they knew they had sinned, so they hid in the garden of Eden. Of course they couldn't hide long from God, who then pronounced the consequences of their disobedience. God had given them the dominion of the whole earth. But by their disobedience, they had sold out to Satan. Now Satan, the evil one, would be prince of the earth.

Yet God, desiring to redeem Adam and Eve (and the rest of humankind which would be born) gave his first promise—the first part of a red thread of redemption that stretches throughout the Bible.

God predicted someone would come from the seed of the woman who would defeat Satan (Gen. 3:15). "I will put enmity between you and the woman, and between your offspring and hers; he will crush your head, and you will strike his heel." This offspring would be the Messiah, the Anointed one.

The Bible reveals, little by little, God's plan to restore humankind to fellowship with himself through this anointed one. When Isaiah calls him a "branch" and a "shoot from the stump of Jesse," he is building on hundreds of years of 'puzzle pieces' that begin to give the Jews a picture of this Messiah. The picture of the Messiah begun in the Garden of Eden continues to take shape through The Law & The Prophets, and finally throughout the New Testament. In these next few pages, we will see how God teaches his people, little by little, about the Messiah.

From the line of Adam and Eve's third son, Seth, after many generations, Noah was born. Noah was a type of Christ in that he was the "only truly righteous man living on the earth at that time,"(Gen. 6:10, LB) and God chose to save a remnant through him. He obediently carried out the long-term commitment to which God had called him—to build the ark. After Noah and his wife and sons (Shem, Ham, and Japheth) and the animals survived the flood, God made a covenant with them. He set the rainbow in the sky as a reminder of that covenant.

About ten generations after Noah, Abram was born from the line of Shem. God called Abram (later renamed Abraham) to be the father of his chosen nation. God said he would bless not only Abraham, but also "I will bless those who bless you...; and by you all the families of the earth shall bless themselves" (Genesis 12:1-3, 22:18).

Yes, God's purpose in choosing the nation of Israel was to bring his plan of salvation to people all over the world. Israel was his chosen instrument through whom he would do this.

God's plan continues throughout the Old Testament with several "types" or foreshadows of Christ to help the chosen nation understand who to look for. Abraham's son, Isaac, became a type of Christ (or picture of the Messiah) when he lay on the altar to be sacrificed by his own father. Genesis 22:8 indicates that Abraham trusted God, though he must have been in anguish wondering why

God would ask him to sacrifice his own son. An angel stopped that sacrifice, and Abraham was commended for his obedience.

Joseph, the son of Jacob, was a type of Christ in that he was unjustly sold into slavery, and unjustly accused, but eventually saved his family from starvation. He forgave his brothers just as Jesus Christ later forgave his murderers.

Four hundred years after Joseph, God chose Moses to rescue his people out of slavery. The Passover lamb before the Exodus is a foreshadow of Jesus, our Paschal lamb who died in our place to rescue us out of the slavery of sin. The reason Jesus rescued us, according to Gal.4:3-7, is so he could adopt us as his very own children.

God continues to teach his people, little by little, what the Messiah is like. In John1:29-31, John the Baptist called Jesus the "Lamb of God who takes away the sin of the world," (John 1:29-31) Maybe he was thinking of Isaiah 53 where Isaiah said he was led like a lamb to the slaughter. Peter also speaks of Christ as a lamb, (I Peter 1:18-19). In The Revelation, the apostle John saw a live lamb that looked like it had been killed, and the angels praised it by singing, "Worthy is the lamb that was slain, (Rev. 5:12).

Later John was told, "They will make war against the Lamb, but the Lamb will overcome them because he is Lord of lords and King of kings—and with him will be his called, chosen and faithful followers," Rev. 17:14.
The Lamb will even be the lamp of the heavenly city, (Revelation 21:23). So this piece of the puzzle connects with those of Messiah being the Light.

The Bible seems to give several parallels between Moses and Jesus:

1.In both lives, a king wanted the babies killed, but they escaped miraculously. Ex.1:15-16 & 2:1-10/Mt.2:13-18):

2.They both fasted in the wilderness 40 days and 40 nights, (Ex.34:28/Mt.4:2).

3.They each commanded the sea and it obeyed, (Ex.14:21/Mt.8:26).

4.In each instance, the Lord provided bread to eat, (Ex.16:15 and Mt.14:13-21).

5.Each one's face was "radiant" or "shone like the sun, (Ex.34:35/Mt.17:2).

6.Each met unbelief in his own family, (Nu.12:2/John 7:5).

7.Each prayed on behalf of those who sinned, (Ex.32:32/Lk23:34).

8.Each had seventy to help with the work (Numbers11:16-17, Luke 10:1).

9.Both sacrificed the Passover Lamb (Ex. 12:3, 7-8, 12-13,/I Corinthians 5:7).

During the Israelites' forty years in the wilderness, God gave them several object lessons which also foreshadowed the coming Messiah. Here are four of them:

1. The rock in the wilderness gave out fresh water for the people to drink, (Exodus 17:6 and Numbers 20:8). Jesus was called the rock,

(see Deut. 32:3, Romans 9:33, and Cor.10:4). Jesus is also the living water, (John.4:10, 7:38)

2. In Numbers, the bronze snake was lifted up with the promise that whoever looked at it in faith would be healed of poisonous snake bites. Jesus said "Just as Moses lifted up the snake in the desert, so the Son of Man must be lifted up, that everyone who believes in him may have eternal life. (John 3:14-15, NIV).

3. Leviticus says that life is in the blood—without the shedding of blood there is no forgiveness of sins. Read Lev. 17:11, Matt. 26:28, Ephesians1:7, 1 Pet.1:18-19, 1Jn.1:7.

4. Numbers 24:17 mentions a "star" that would come out of Jacob and conquer Israel's enemies. The wise men probably knew of this prophecy, therefore followed the star of Bethlehem to find the baby Jesus. 2 Peter 1:19 and Revelation 22:16 call Jesus the morning star.

Other people foreshadowed Christ, besides those "types of Christ" we previously noted: In Deuteronomy.18:17-19, Moses told the Israelites that God would raise up a prophet like him from among the Israelites and that they must listen to him.

Boaz, kinsman redeemer to Ruth, foreshadowed Christ, who is our kinsman-redeemer. (Ruth 4:13-22). His great-grandson became King David.

God called King David a man after his own heart. Even though he sinned, he sincerely repented and the usual attitude of his heart was love for God and obedience to him. God promised him one of his descendants would reign over God's kingdom forever (1Chronicles17:14 NIV).

After David's reign, many prophecies refer to the promised Messiah, who would come from the line of David and one day reign on David's throne. Isaiah 9:7, and 11:2 say he will be a king of peace, justice and righteousness and that the Spirit of the Lord will rest on him.

With the outline of this puzzle completed, other prophecies fill in the center of the puzzle of what this Messiah will be like:

- The anointed one will eventually rule over all nations, (Psalm 2:8-9).
- He would not remain in the grave. (Psalm16:10-11).
- He will be excellent and gracious; his throne will last forever (Psalm 45:2 and 6).
- He would ascend, leading captives, (Psalm 68:18).
- Psalm 69:21, They would give him vinegar to drink,
- Psalm 118:22, Messiah would be rejected, but then will become the capstone, which means the most important.
- Psalm 132:11, Messiah would be a descendant of David.
- Isaiah 7:14, Messiah, born of a virgin, would be "God with us" (Immanuel).
- Isaiah 2:4, Isaiah prophecies a reign of peace by the Lord.
- Isaiah 9:2, The Light of the World would live in the area of Naphtali and Zebulun (Galilee). He would be called "Wonderful Counselor, Mighty God, Everlasting Father, Prince of Peace."

This King of Peace would come from the line of David, Jesse's son, bringing in a righteous kingdom. The Spirit of the LORD would rest on him.

The promises continue throughout scripture. They help us understand better the salvation God planned. Messiah would be *"the lamb of God who takes away the sin of the world."* (John 1:29)

The day is coming when the world system *"will make war against the Lamb, but the Lamb will overcome them because he is Lord of lords and King of kings—and with him will be his called, chosen, and faithful followers."* This promise is in Revelation 17:14 and completes the Red Thread of Redemption. The world system will fall and Jesus will reign forever!

Then we who belong to him will be with him in Heaven forever! Hallelujah!

Prayer: Thank you Father for your wonderful plan of salvation. Thank you for sending your Son, our Messiah, Jesus Christ, to reconcile us to yourself.

In Jesus name, Amen.

Chapter Six
Thanks and Praise

"You will say in that day: "I will give thanks to thee, O LORD, for though thou wast angry with me, thy anger turned away and thou didst comfort me. Behold, God is my salvation; I will trust, and will not be afraid; for the LORD God is my strength and my song, and he has become my salvation." (Isaiah 12:1 and 2 RSV).

"With joy you will draw water from the wells of salvation, and you will say in that day: "Give thanks to the LORD, call upon his name: make known his deeds among the nations, proclaim that his *name is exalted. Sing praises to the LORD, for he has done gloriously; let this be known in all the earth; Shout, and sing for joy, O inhabitant of Zion, for great in your midst is the Holy One of Israel."* (Isaiah 12:3–6, RSV)

Thank you, Lord, that you don't leave nations or individuals in the messes we get ourselves into, but mercifully rescue and redeem us. We praise you for providing the spiritual armor and weapons we need to fight the battle against Satan and his forces.

In your name, Lord Jesus, I put on the belt of truth, for *you are the way, the truth, the life;* in you all things hold together. I accept your righteousness as my breastplate, and put on the shoes that enable me to walk in peace, spreading the gospel of peace.

In your name I put on the helmet of salvation, for *"I know whom I have believed, and am convinced that he is able to guard what I've entrusted to him"* (2 Tim. 1:12). Thank you also for the shield of faith—that you are a shield about me—and for the sword of the Spirit which is the Word of God. I will use them to fight like Jesus did. In Jesus' name, Amen.

Following are two poems I wrote during and after my "runaway period."

Prayer of Confusion

Will somebody teach me how to live?
What is the secret? How do I give?
How do I yield my heart?

Will somebody tell me who I am?
Which is the truth and which but a sham?
How did deception start?

What are the answers? I need them now
to questions I can't figure out somehow.
Am I wise or am I a fool? Am I loving or am I cruel?
How do I listen and who will speak?
I feel confused and amazingly weak.

Oh LORD, take control of my inner soul.
Where I am lacking, please make me whole.
Search me and make me true.

For you are the One who gave me life!
Tell me the secret, thus end my strife.
Teach me to live for You!

By Judith Vander Wege

Lord, Be the Ruler

Lord, be the ruler of my heart. I yield the throne to Thee.
I pray no selfishness nor pride nor treasures that I see
usurp the throne or take command to lead my flesh astray.
May you be King, and Lord of all that's in my life today.

Lord, be the ruler of my soul. My thoughts, so often wrong,
can keep me out of touch with you. The devil's pull is strong.
Yet, stronger still, your pull of love has led me here today
to ask you, Lord, to take control. Yes, be my King today.

By Judith Vander Wege